I, SU

MW00883345

THE ART OF WAR FOR KIDS

First Edition

Text © Martin Malchev

Illustrations © Martin Malchev

m.k.malchev@gmail.com

Contents

Introduction

Greetings, young warriors! Good to see you! My name is General Sun Tzu, and I am here to teach you all about the art of winning. But first, let me introduce myself. I was born in the heartland of ancient China a long, long time ago. In my lifetime, I have seen and participated in many wars, and believe me when I tell you that they are terrible. Wars cause so much suffering and destruction. And what's worse, they result in the loss of precious human lives. For the sake of humanity, we must do our best to avoid them. But sometimes, they are unavoidable. Like, when someone is defending their life and freedom. Although all of them are horrendous experiences, some have a just and righteous cause. In these cases, it is essential to stand your ground and protect what's right. In such difficult times, heroes and great leaders emerge.

Every hero and every good general knows that the first thing one must do is try to avoid bloodshed. They should do this through negotiations or other means. As I often say:

"The supreme art of war is to subdue the enemy without fighting."

The goal is to win without actually battling. Instead, we must strive to achieve our goals with minimal destruction and high efficiency. There are many ways to do this, and I will teach you all of them.

But don't get me wrong, my friends. Even if you avoid an actual battle, the war is still on. We just change how we fight. We replace the battlefield with the negotiating table. Or we use clever strategies to outwit our opponents and win without physically harming them.

Listen to me, young warriors, when I tell you this: Wars are the most extreme form of conflict, yet conflicts are inevitable in life. It is because they are part of human nature and of nature in general. Not only humans but animals and even plants fight and compete with each other. Many members of the animal kingdom hunt to survive. Males of the same species, such as lions and deer, often fight for the attention of females and the right to father their young. Even trees compete for sunlight. Those that grow more cast a shadow over their rivals, hindering their development. Did you know that even some plants hunt? They eat bugs and small animals.

We can see milder forms of rivalry in sports, business, school, or between siblings. Such rivalry is called competition, and it is usually a good thing. It can drive innovation, improvement, and adaptation. Whether it is war, sports, or sibling quarrels, the best solution is to win without fighting.

"But General Tzu, isn't it best to avoid conflicts altogether?" - you may ask. And my answer is *"NO!"*. Yes, you can try to avoid them. Actually, I urge you to do so, as long as it doesn't hurt you. But the thing is, your good intentions won't matter if your opponent doesn't share your views. And they usually don't. Trying to end a conflict unilaterally is like deciding not to kick the ball during a soccer game. Your unwillingness to participate doesn't stop the game. It even makes it easier for your opponent to win. Imagine two boxers. One throws punches, and the other doesn't. Who would win? If the one who is not punching decides to leave the

ring, who wins? The one who stands and the one who punches—that's who.

Now that I have explained why you should win, I must teach you how to do it. And here you are in luck because I have been doing this for centuries. I even wrote an entire book on winning, and it's the best seller in that category.

"But General Sun, what do your ancient teachings have to do with me?" - you may ask. Well, young warriors, much like the rivers

and mountains of our world, human nature has stayed the same throughout time. Competition, conflict, and the principles of winning are as relevant today as they were in my time.

We will talk about strategy —not just in war but in sports, in your studies, and in dealing with your friends and siblings. You will learn how important it is to know yourself and your rivals. You will also discover the power of wisdom and patience. I will share stories from the past, full of lessons that have stood the test of time. Together, we will draw parallels with your world. We will find ways to apply age-old wisdom to the challenges you face. We will explore the true meaning of victory. It is not just about winning battles. It's about overcoming obstacles with courage, intelligence, and compassion.

So gear up, young friends, and let me turn you into true winners.

Your favorite general,

Sun Tzu

Chapter 1
The Art of Strategic Planning

Good day, cadets! Please take your seats on the mats in this beautiful courtyard of our traditional Chinese school. Here, under the shade of the ginkgo tree[1], I will teach you about the art

---

[1] *The Ginkgo tree* (*Ginkgo biloba*) is one of the oldest tree species in the world. It's often called a "living fossil" because it's the only surviving member of an ancient group of trees dating back more than 270 million years. It has unique fan-shaped leaves that turn bright yellow in the fall. Ginkgo trees are robust and can live for thousands of years. People in China have grown these trees for centuries. They use the seeds and leaves to make medicine. Ginkgo trees are also popular in cities. They can withstand pollution and aren't easily affected by insects and diseases. This makes them great for planting along streets and in parks.

of strategic planning. *"What is strategy, General Sun?"* - you may ask. Strategy, my dear warriors, is your plan for overcoming obstacles and achieving your goals. It applies on the battlefield, in your classroom, or even at home.

Let's take our school as an example and discuss how and why it came to be. First, someone realized that society would benefit if it consisted of intelligent and wise individuals. So, educating the people became his goal. Then, he began to think about how to achieve it. He decided to build a place of education. Bright minds like you could gather there to share knowledge and wisdom. That was his strategy for achieving the goal.

Next, he needed a detailed step-by-step plan outlining exactly how to build the school. Where to place it. How to obtain a building permit. What kind of building to construct. How to pay for it. Where to find good teachers like myself. All these and many more steps of action required careful planning. That is tactics.

In summary, strategy is the plan to achieve a longer-term, larger-scale goal. Tactics are the specific actions you take to carry out the strategy.

Do you understand, young scholars? No? OK, let me give you another example. Imagine you are playing chess. Each move you make is not just about moving a piece. It's about thinking ahead. You must predict your opponent's next moves and prepare your path to victory. That is strategy. Tactics are the specific actions you take. They are the individual moves in the game. Each is carefully calculated to contribute to your strategy.

Strategy and tactics differ in their scope and time frame. Strategy is the general plan designed to achieve a big goal. It is long-term. It involves setting goals and determining what actions to take to achieve them. It also requires mobilizing resources to carry out the actions. Tactics are the specific actions or steps you take to realize the strategy. They are short-term, flexible, and can adapt to current conditions.

Remember this:

"Strategy without tactics is the slowest route to victory. Tactics without strategy is the noise before defeat."

This quote of mine highlights the need to balance your big plan (the strategy) with the steps you take to reach it (the tactics).

Let's go back to the example of our beautiful school. Imagine what it would have looked like if we had only the idea to build it. But, we had no architectural plans, building materials, plot of land, permits, teachers, or even students. Would such a strategy work? Hardly. Now, picture having all the necessary resources but lacking a plan (strategy) for constructing a school. How would that work?

I have taught you about strategy and tactics. Now, let me share an incredible story from old times to clarify these concepts. It is the true story of the Battle of Agincourt.

It all happened in 1415, during a time known as the Hundred Years' War. In these turbulent times, King Henry V of England and his army were on the brink of a great battle. His brave soldiers were weary from long marches, scarce food, and the chill of an unforgiving autumn. They were far from home and facing a French force nearly five times their size.

The French knights, clad in shining armor, were bold and many. Confident of victory, they were closing in on their enemy like a massive iron wave. It seemed as though all was lost for the English. But King Henry refused to accept his fate. Instead, he devised a plan that relied more on superior strategy than on strength. He chose a slender strip of battlefield nestled between two dense forests. This choice was no accident. The woods would serve as a natural barrier, funneling the mighty French army into a narrow corridor. There, their numbers would count for nothing.

As dawn broke, a fog hung low over the field at Agincourt. The English longbowmen, a band of brothers in arms, took up positions on the flanks. Their bows were tall, and their arrows sharp. Each feathered shaft was ready to sing through the air. At a signal from King Henry, a massive volley of arrows soared high into the sky. They blotted out the sun and rained down like a storm on the French knights. The arrows were relentless and accurate. They pierced armor and flesh as the French army trudged through the muck of the wet field.

The once proud cavalry found themselves stuck in the mud. Their heavy armor became their prison as they struggled to advance. The narrow pass, cleverly chosen by King Henry, turned the battle into a chaotic mess for the French. Their numbers, usually an advantage, were now a hindrance. The knights crowded together tightly on the muddy field. They couldn't maneuver. Their heavy steps turned the ground into a quagmire. The French were confused. The English archers continued their deadly dance. Arrows whistled through the air, each one singing a song of defiance. The French knights, bewildered and beset on all sides by the stinging arrows of the English, began to falter.

King Henry, seeing the tide turning, rallied his foot soldiers. *"Onward, brave hearts!"* - he shouted, drawing his sword and leading the charge. Their king's courage inspired the English soldiers. They rushed forward, steel in hand, to meet the stalled French knights. The battle raged like a fierce storm. The narrow field was a swirl of clashing swords, flying arrows, and the cries of men. The French, unable to use their superior numbers, fell into disarray. The English advance was relentless. It trapped many in the mud, unable to escape.

The sun was setting over Agincourt. The field was covered with the fallen, and the once mighty French army was in retreat. King Henry's clever plan turned an inevitable defeat into a stunning victory. The English soldiers, exhausted but triumphant, cheered their king. Henry walked among them, clapping shoulders and praising their bravery. Together, they faced a giant and emerged victorious. They won not by brute force but by the sharpness of their minds and the strength of their spirits.

Thus, the Battle of Agincourt became a legend. People told and retold it. It was a tale of how wisdom, courage, and a bit of English weather could turn the tide of history. This story demonstrates the power of good strategy and tactics, which triumph even in the face of significant challenges.

King Henry's strategy was to use the terrain to nullify the French numerical advantage and secure victory. His tactics were the specific actions he took, such as where he positioned his soldiers and when they attacked.

In your life, strategic planning is equally important. Say you have a big project in school. Do not dive in without a plan. Break it down. Understand the challenges. Gather your resources. Then, step forward. It is like preparing for a big game or performance. Understand your strengths, recognize your weaknesses, and plan accordingly. Remember, young warriors. Strategic planning is about seeing the big picture. It is about understanding that each step is part of your journey to victory. Embrace this art, and you will be ready for the challenges ahead. You will also get prepared for a life of purpose and accomplishment.

In our ancient Chinese school, it is tradition to ponder and discuss what we learn from each lesson. So, my curious students, let me ask you a few questions to contemplate. What are the "battles" you face in your daily life? And how can you use strategic planning to overcome them? Think about it and jot down your thoughts in a notebook. If you make this a habit, it will greatly benefit your life in the future. Planning is the first step to winning.

Class dismissed.

Chapter 2

Know Yourself

認
識
你
自
己

Greetings, young strategists! Welcome back to our beautiful school. The weather is sunny, so let's go outside the classroom again. We'll have our lesson in the courtyard, under the ginkgo trees near the pond. Put your mats on the wooden deck and sit comfortably. Relax. Calm your curious minds and look at those beautiful mountains in the distance. There! Right above the pitched tile roof of our wooden school building. Serene scenery, isn't it? Looks so peaceful that it predisposes to meditation and relaxation.

That's how we see it from here. But if you go there, you will see it is full of life, action, and competition. Predators hunt there. Birds build nests. Trees compete for the light of the sun. Herbivores eat the plants, but other plants rise to replace them. After dusk, nocturnal animals come out and do their thing. Nature is so calm and so busy at the same time.

Now, my dear apprentices, imagine you are animals living in these same mountains. Let's say that you are a monkey, and you are facing a lion. Would you fight him? No? Why not? Now imagine that you have to fight the lion in the jungle, but you are a smart monkey: you remember that, unlike the lion, you have hands. You can throw stones at him while you are safe on a tree. You can strike him from a distance with a long, sharp stick. And you can set all kinds of traps for him while he can't.

Do you think you can win now? I do. Because it's not about who is stronger, but who knows themselves better. I often tell my students:

"Know yourself, and you will win all battles."

Today's lesson is about understanding who you are, your strengths, and your weaknesses. This self-awareness is your greatest ally in any challenge you face. Knowing yourself is like having a map during a journey. It shows you where you are, the terrain you can easily navigate, and the paths you may find challenging. This knowledge is powerful. It's not about boasting of your strengths or feeling disheartened by your weaknesses. Instead, it's about honest reflection, continuous learning, and growth.

There is an old story from my days that I'd like to share with you. Some say it's a legend, while others believe it to be true. Regardless, the story is good and very instructive. So, listen up.

In the Warring States era, a young warrior named Liang was renowned throughout the land. He was known for his unparalleled bravery and strength. In every village and town, they whispered his name in awe. He was said to have never suffered defeat in battle. Liang was tall and mighty. His muscles were as tough as the steel of his sword. His eyes burned with fierce determination. His presence alone could turn the tide of battle.

Liang's biggest challenge was not to be found on the battlefield but within his own heart. For all his physical strength, Liang was easily provoked to anger. A harsh word, a disdainful look, or even a perceived slight could ignite a fiery temper. It burned uncontrollably within him. His enemies, cunning and observant, soon learned to exploit this weakness. They realized that a warrior consumed by rage was a warrior who could be defeated.

The turning point for Liang came during a major battle. It threatened the very existence of his homeland. The enemy, a rival state known for its astute tactics, had laid a trap for him. Amid the fray, the opposing general sent forth a challenger: a warrior who taunted and jeered at Liang. His words were so cutting that they pierced deeper than any sword. Liang was enraged. He charged forward, forgetting his strategy and abandoning his discipline. The battle raged around him. It was a maelstrom of chaos. With vision blurred by rage, Liang could only see his taunter. His strikes were powerful but wild, his defense - neglected.

It was then, in his blind fury, that Liang stumbled into the enemy's trap. He was severely wounded and fell unconscious as his army got routed. His enemies thought he was dead and continued their conquest. But Liang survived, thanks to his robust physique and an incredible stroke of luck. He made his way to a Buddhist monastery on a nearby mountain. The monks healed Liang's wounds, but his spirit was far more broken than his body. Defeated and humiliated, he carried the heavy burden of his failure. Many days and nights passed as Liang wallowed in self-pity.

One afternoon, he stumbled upon a great book in the monastery library. It was called *The Art of War*, written by the wise sage that is I. Yes, my timeless, bestselling classic. You should read it as well. In it, Liang read that the most crucial trait of a true champion is self-awareness. At that moment, a spark of wisdom kindled. Liang began to reflect and self-analyze. And then, it struck him all at once. He realized that his quick temper was his greatest weakness and that he needed to learn how to control it.

But like any new and unfamiliar challenge, it was difficult for him, so he sought help. He turned to the monks and asked for guidance on controlling his anger, thoughts, and emotions. Remember, my fellow warriors! Whenever you face a challenge, it's always a good idea to seek help or advice. Whatever difficulty you face, someone else has already overcome it. In most cases, they would be happy to lend you a hand. Great rulers always seek the wisdom of good advisors. Great warriors are always glad to face their battles accompanied by trusted allies.

Back to our story. The monks taught Liang to meditate, to still the waters of his mind, and to see the world with clarity and calm. As the seasons changed, so did Liang. He returned to his people not just as a warrior of physical might but also as a leader of serene strength. When the next battle came, his enemies found no weakness to exploit. There was no anger to provoke. Liang led his army with a calm as unyielding as the mountains. His strategies were as baffling as a labyrinth of mirrors. Ultimately, it wasn't Liang's sword that secured victory; it was his newfound wisdom. He had learned that the fiercest battles are fought not against the world but in the depths of one's soul. By mastering himself, he had become genuinely unbeatable.

Today, when I think of people who became winners by assessing their traits, I think of Lionel Messi. This world-renowned soccer player encountered some serious challenges during his youth.

They included a medical condition. Messi was diagnosed with a growth hormone deficiency when he was about eleven years old. This condition affected his growth. It left him much smaller and less developed than his peers. His short stature and weak muscles were a significant disadvantage for an athlete. Especially for the sport that he loved so much. But he didn't give in to despair. Instead, he took stock of his strengths and weaknesses. Then, based on that assessment, he developed a strategy and took action. Messi realized his short height allowed him to change direction faster than taller defenders. He decided to cultivate this skill and use it to his advantage. Long story short, he has become the best dribbler and one of the greatest soccer players in history. His story shows how understanding and using your unique traits can lead to great success.

A good understanding of your skills can help you contribute more effectively when working on a team project. In sports, understanding your body can help you train more effectively. The same goes for your hobbies. Understanding your interests and strengths can lead to remarkable creations.

But remember my dear disciples, knowing yourself isn't a one-time task. It's a journey, an ongoing process of growth and discovery. Each challenge and every new experience teaches you more about who you are and who you can become. Knowing oneself is the second step in the art of winning, not just in battles but in the grand adventure of life.

Now, let's go back to the meditation we nearly started at the beginning of this lesson. *"What is meditation, General Sun?"* - you ask. Good question, my curious scholars. Meditation is when you sit quietly, take deep breaths, and try not to focus on anything specific. While doing this, thoughts will still come to you. Instead of trying to block them, aim to simply acknowledge them without dwelling on them. Like a bystander, you should strive to be aware of everything without attachment. If it helps, you can focus on your breathing, relaxing music, a repeated sound, or a sensation in your body. These can serve as anchors. When you notice you're paying too much attention to a particular thought, gently refocus on your anchor and return to your observing state.

The goal is to clear your mind of attachments, because they prevent you from seeing things clearly and impartially. It's like giving your brain a little vacation. You'll feel rejuvenated, and good ideas will come to you much more easily. I recommend adding meditation to your schedule. You will greatly benefit if you manage to turn it into a habit.

So, do you want to try meditating right now? Let's do it!

Sit still. Breathe deeply and slowly. Focus on your breathing. When a thought arises, just acknowledge it and let it go. If you find yourself paying attention to a thought, gently refocus on your breathing. Do this for as long as you feel comfortable and relaxed. Well, that's it. It wasn't too hard, right? It's important to note that meditation compounds over time. It's like anything else: The more you do it, the better you become.

Now that you've finished your meditation and your mind is clearer, I want you to contemplate your self-awareness. Ask yourself: What are your strengths, and how can you use them to overcome the challenges you face? What are your weaknesses? How can you mitigate them, or even turn them into advantages? Get to know yourself better, because this is the second step to winning.

We'll meet again in the next lesson.

Class dismissed.

Chapter 3

Know Your Enemy

Greetings, brave ones! Today, we will talk about the importance of knowing your enemies. Please take your places on your mats, and let's begin the lesson. Wait! What is that in the sky? Oh, it's a flock of Red-crowned Cranes[1]. They return

---

[1] **The Red-crowned Crane** is known for its distinctive look. It is one of the largest crane species. You can spot it by its white body, black neck and tail, and a red patch on its head. Many Asian cultures revere these birds as symbols of luck, long life, and loyalty. They are most common in East Asia, especially in China and Japan. They live in marshes, on riverbanks, and in wetlands. Despite their fame, Red-crowned Cranes are endangered. This is due to habitat loss, human disturbance, and environmental changes. Efforts to protect these majestic birds are ongoing.

to build their nests and raise their young, as they do every spring. What majestic creatures they are! Did you know that in Chinese culture, they symbolize longevity and immortality? That may be because they are great survivors. They rarely fall prey to even the fiercest predators.

"How do they do that, General Sun Tzu?" - you may ask. They do it by knowing their enemies exceptionally well. Red-crowned Cranes know that some predators can snatch their eggs or chicks while others will not. For example, they are not afraid of predators like harriers, falcons, and owls. Cranes know what those carnivores can and can not do.

On the other hand, cranes stay vigilant for eagles, red foxes, wolves, weasels, badgers, and raccoon dogs. They do this for the same reason—they know these predators well. So well, in fact, that they have developed different strategies for each one. For example, if a red fox is nearing their nest and about to catch their chicks, the cranes will act accordingly. Foxes prefer to hunt weak and sick animals. Knowing this, the adult crane will come close enough for the fox to see it. Then, it will pretend that its foot and wing are broken, limping away from the nest and flapping its wings erratically. The crane's apparent vulnerability lures the predator away from the nest. It draws it toward the adult bird, which appears to be an easier target. Once the predator is far from the nest, the crane will miraculously "recover" and fly away. That leaves the predator confused and the nest safe.

Red-crowned Cranes know that some of their most dangerous enemies can't swim. That is why they build their nests in wetlands, marshes, and rivers. Cranes hide their nests in tall reeds to avoid being spotted by sharp-eyed predators. Sometimes, they even build fake nests and pretend to inhabit them to decoy carnivores. Their actual nests, with their eggs, are safe elsewhere. Cranes also know that they need to be very quiet when some predators are around and loud in the presence of others. They even adapt their fighting style to their enemy when battle becomes unavoidable. And when cranes see a predator that is too powerful, they even call for reinforcements. Their knowledge of their enemies is that good. That is why the cranes always win.

I often say:

"If you know the enemy and know yourself, you need not fear the result of a hundred battles."

This principle applies not only to wars but to any form of rivalry.

Take sports, for example. Basketball fans know LeBron James not only for his physical prowess but also for his mental game. James doesn't just watch game tapes of his opponents. He delves into their strategies, strengths, and weaknesses. It's like he is dissecting their game, piece by piece, to understand how they tick. This knowledge allows him to adapt his play style, make quick decisions, and lead his team to victory.

In the business world, Elon Musk's success with Tesla Motors is another example. The auto industry's shift toward electric vehicles (EVs) has been slow. Watching this, Musk saw an opportunity to innovate. His company, Tesla Motors, focused on making electric cars. They also worked on building an ecosystem around EVs, including charging stations and battery technology. Musk understood the auto industry's weaknesses, which enabled him to turn Tesla into a leader in the EV market.

You see, my dear disciples - studying your opponent is crucial for victory. But this understanding isn't about fostering hatred or fear. It's about understanding and seeing the world through another's eyes. Like a master Go[2] player, you must anticipate your opponent's moves. Understanding your rival allows you to act with wisdom and foresight. Your "enemy" could be a real person or an obstacle you face. By knowing them, you prepare for the

---

[2] **Go** is an ancient board game that originated in China over 4,000 years ago. This makes it one of the oldest games still played today. It's played with black and white stones on a grid of lines (usually 19x19). Players take turns placing their stones on the board. They try to surround and capture each other's pieces and control more territory. Go is easy to learn but can be incredibly complex and strategic. That is why it's often compared to chess, although the rules differ. It is popular worldwide for teaching patience and strategic thinking.

challenges ahead. You also open doors to empathy, respect, and effective conflict resolution. When you put yourself in your rival's shoes, you see the situation from their point of view. You can grasp the root of the problem and find solutions that benefit both sides. And that is the ultimate victory: A situation where both sides win without actually fighting.

Such a thing happened back in my days. There were two kingdoms on the brink of war. Each had its strengths, each its weaknesses. But one king chose to learn instead of boasting and shouting threats. He studied his adversary's language. He explored their culture, tactics, terrain, and much more. Thanks to this, the king understood his foe's fears, concerns, and goals. He saw the situation from another perspective. This newfound knowledge caused him to alter his strategy. Instead of preparing his army for grueling battles, he prepared the negotiating table for long debates. And when the talks began, he engaged with respect and compassion. The result? Peace, which lasted for generations. All because the king knew his enemy.

In your life, this principle has many faces. It could be understanding a classmate whom you dislike or who bothers you. Or it could mean grasping a complex subject that feels like a formidable foe. When you play sports, it's about knowing the strengths and weaknesses of the opposing team. It even applies to understanding your siblings, with whom you may have your daily little battles.

Hear my advice, young warriors! Try to develop the habit of studying your rivals and putting yourself in their shoes. Learn as much as possible about them, then try to think as they think. This habit alone will help you tremendously to become a true winner in life. Knowing your enemy is the third step to winning.

As we near the end of our lesson, I want you to think about a "battle" you're currently facing. How can you understand the other side better? How can this insight guide your actions and thoughts? Will you use this knowledge to crush your enemy? Or will you strive for the ultimate victory where both sides win without clashing?

Contemplate these questions during the break.

Class dismissed.

Chapter 4

The Art of Winning Without Fighting

Hello, young warriors! It's great to be with you again! I can see that your thirst for knowledge is immense, so let's try to quench it. But first, let's go inside the classroom, for the day is cloudy and about to pour. Hey, you two! Light those lanterns that hang from the ceiling beams. The rest of you, take your places on your mats, facing towards me.

I notice a few new students, so allow me to reintroduce myself. My name is General Sun Tzu. I am a teacher, a philosopher, a military commander, a bestselling author, and overall a nice guy. My field of expertise is winning. Winning wars, winning battles, winning in sports, winning in business, winning in your relationships, and winning in general.

Who will read the text on that bamboo slip hanging on the wall behind me? Everyone raises their hand. Nice! OK, you, with the green Hanfu[1] garment. Can you read it out loud, please? Yes, thank you! It says:

"The greatest victory is that which requires no battle."

Think about it! Why would you bother to fight if you can win without fighting? In every battle, there is a risk of losing. Why take chances if you can ensure your victory by other means? *"What other means?"* - you ask. Means such as intelligence and espionage, psychological warfare, strategic flexibility, diplomacy and alliances, economic warfare, demonstration of superiority,

---

[1] *Hanfu* refers to the traditional clothing of the Han Chinese, the ethnic majority in China. This fabulous dress style has been around for over three thousand years. It includes a cross-collared robe or shirt and a long skirt or trousers. They are often paired with a belt. The design of the Hanfu can vary a lot. It depends on the wearer's status, the occasion, and the dynasty during which it was worn. Hanfu garments are known for their elegant, flowing style. They show the depth of Chinese culture and aesthetics. In ancient times, these garments were not just clothes. They were a symbol of culture and values. The revival of Hanfu shows a growing interest in traditional culture among the Chinese. It serves as a means to connect with their heritage and history.

and indirect approaches.

Sounds complicated? Don't worry. I'll explain them in a way that even your pet would understand. These methods may also sound boring to some, but actually, they are pretty cool. Allow me to clarify each of them in the context of military strategy. Then, we will discuss how we can apply them in our daily lives. So here they are:

Intelligence and Espionage

Gathering intelligence about the enemy's plans, strengths, and weaknesses is vital during warfare. Understanding your enemy allows you to exploit their weaknesses before resorting to combat.

For our daily life example, imagine you are running for a student council position in high school.

Scenario 1: You just apply like everyone else and hope and pray that they choose you.

Scenario 2: You use the principle of Intelligence and Espionage. You research and assess the environment. You get to know your potential voters. Gather intelligence on their concerns, interests, and needs. Observe common complaints on social media or note issues raised in class discussions. Learn about the campaign promises, strengths, and weaknesses of your rivals. What are they offering, and how do their goals align with the student's needs? Find out which social media platforms your classmates prefer and how they use them. What are the things they share, what they like, and what they don't like? Talk to your classmates in person whenever possible. It will help you learn more about their wants and needs and what your competitors offer. Then, use this info to craft a winning campaign. Your classmates should relate to it, for it will promise better solutions to their problems than your opponents.

Which of these two scenarios is more likely to achieve your goal? Do you see now why gathering intelligence is vital for winning?

Psychological Warfare

The goal here is to affect your opponent's morale and psychological state. This may involve spreading misinformation to confuse or demoralize the enemy during the war. Or using propaganda[2] to undermine their will to fight. The aim is to win by causing chaos and disarray within the enemy's ranks.

As an example from civilian life, let me share a funny trick used by the world-famous bodybuilder, actor, and governor - Arnold Schwarzenegger. He used to play it on his opponents during bodybuilding competitions. Right before their performance, Arnold would walk up to them and ask with a concerned look if

---

[2] *Propaganda* is information used to promote a particular political cause or opinion. It is often biased or misleading. It can spread through media like TV, radio, the Internet, and newspapers. Its purpose is to influence people's opinions.

they were feeling all right. Then, he would tell them they looked sick and tired. He would ask them what had happened to their arm or back muscles. *"They used to be bigger."* - he would say. In this way, Arnold sowed the seeds of self-doubt, which overtook his rivals. Their insecurity affected their performance, and it made Arnold's job much easier. He won the Mr. Olympia title seven times.

Strategic Flexibility

In warfare, this means adapting to the situation and being unpredictable. Again, the goal is to win without a fight. It may require changing plans at the last minute to catch the enemy off guard. Or using deception to make the enemy think you are weak when you are strong and strong when you are weak. Genghis Khan's Mongol army used many such strategies. One was to pretend to be weak and retreat. Their enemy would start to chase, only to fall into a trap. At other times, the Mongols would light numerous campfires at night. This created the illusion of a much larger force. That caused their foes to overestimate the size of their army and flee.

Speaking about the Mongols, another great story featuring them is The Cats and Birds Siege. According to the legend, Genghis Khan was besieging a city that was proving difficult to capture. Its defenses were strong, and a direct assault would have been costly. Instead of attacking, the great Khan made an unusual offer to the city's inhabitants. He asked them to surrender a large number of cats and birds, in exchange for lifting the siege. The people, thinking it was a strange but harmless request, agreed.

Genghis Khan then did something unexpected. He tied small pieces of cloth to the tails of the cats and birds and set the fabric on fire. The frightened animals ran back to their homes in the stronghold, with their tails burning. As they fled, the fire spread to the houses and buildings. Soon, the whole city was ablaze, and the people inside panicked. With the city weakened by the fire, Genghis Khan's army captured it with ease.

Using strategic flexibility, the mighty Mongols won many victories with little to no fighting. Can you think of ways to use this principle in your life? Maybe you can fool your rivals to make them underestimate or overestimate you. Or you can surprise them and ruin their plans by being unpredictable.

Diplomacy and Alliances

We can use diplomacy and form alliances to outsmart our rivals. With help from others, we can isolate our enemy. This will strengthen our position without fighting.

Imagine that a bully is bothering you at school. What if you allied with six other kids and confronted the bully together? Would the bully continue to bother you? Most likely he would back down without a fight. That is the power of alliances.

Now, picture that you and your sibling are getting a new bunk bed. But you both want the top bunk. Instead of fighting over it, what if you offer your sibling something in exchange? It can be something they want and that you don't really care much about. In this way, you will get what you want, they will get what they want, and you will avoid fighting. That's the power of diplomacy.

Economic Warfare

Wars are costly. They rely heavily on the constant inflow of money, resources, and weapons. That's why attacking the enemy's economy and supply lines can lead to victory without direct combat. The goal is to deplete the enemy's resources and make it hard for them to support their army.

Imagine that you and your team are about to play in the finals of a paintball championship. Somehow, you manage to hide the battle gear of the other team. Do you think they would still want to compete?

Examples like this one may seem a bit odd. It's because of the difference between a real war and most other forms of competition. There are fewer rules in war than in everyday life. In war, we have real adversaries who think ill of us. And in everyday life, we face problems, rivals, or competitors rather than true enemies. For example, your opponents in sports competitions want to win, but they don't really want you to get hurt. Remember that, be good and follow ethical norms. And why not state laws as well...

Back to our principles.

Demonstrating Superiority

The display of overwhelming power can scare your opponent. It can make them retreat or surrender to avoid a losing battle.

Imagine tomorrow you have to participate in a boxing match. Now imagine that you just learned you will be facing Mike Tyson. You know he knocked out 44 of the best heavyweight boxers in the world, many of them in the first round. Would you still want to fight? I know I wouldn't. That is how it feels to know that your opponent is vastly superior. And that is how your rivals must see you if you want to use the principle of Demonstrating Superiority on them.

Indirect Approaches

This method includes attacking the enemy where they are unprepared, or appearing where you are not expected. Instead of engaging in head-on confrontation, target the enemy's weak points.

An excellent example of applying indirect approaches is Hannibal's invasion of the Roman Republic. Hannibal Barca was a Carthaginian general during a period of war with Rome, known as the Second Punic War. At that time, Rome was the greater power. So, everyone expected battles to take place in the neutral waters of the Mediterranean. Or near the border. Or even on Carthaginian land. To their surprise, General Hannibal took the war deep into Roman territory. He not only invaded but managed to do it during the winter. Hannibal used a secret mountain pass in the hard-to-reach Alpine mountains. He was the least expected there. To the horror of the Romans, he even managed to bring war elephants from Africa. And his surprise tactics didn't end there. While conquering Italy, Hannibal encountered large and well-fortified Roman fortresses. Instead of besieging them, Hannibal just went around them. Or he lured the defenders outside the walls, where he crushed them. When Hannibal encountered the main Roman army, he tricked it. The cunning Cartage general got it to fight on terrain where its numbers were at a disadvantage. When the Romans realized Hannibal would defeat them, they tried to flee. But they were horrified to find their escape route cut off. Thanks to the Indirect Approaches principle, Hannibal crushed the Romans. He did it so badly that they were afraid to face him on the battlefield for years.

Let's return to our imaginary scenario where you had to confront Mike Tyson. What if you still have to face him but you can decide where, when, and how? Instead of the boxing ring, you can challenge him to a round of your favorite video game. Or at something that you are great at but he is not. You may be good at chess. Why not defy him on the chess board instead of in the ring? And what if you can get him to play blindfolded, with no hands, and while he is asleep? Would Iron Mike stand a chance against you if you find a way to change the circumstances? To be able to apply the principle of Indirect Approaches, you need to do just that. Change the circumstances in your favor by finding and exploiting your opponent's weaknesses. I admit it: The scenario where you had to play chess against a blindfolded, handcuffed, and sleeping Mike Tyson may be a little unrealistic.

But I bet you know a thing or two about the weak spots of your siblings. Or of some people in the opposing sports team. Or of your rivals at school. The knowledge I just gave you is a powerful weapon, so I hope these people don't get in your way. And I remind you once again that our rivals in everyday life are not really our enemies. Even when we compete with them, it is a friendly competition. Not a battle of life and death. Remember this. Knowledge is power, but power comes with responsibility.

All right, my dear scholars. I told you all that I know about the seven ways to win without fighting. Contemplate them, and I will meet you in the next lesson.

Class dismissed.

Chapter 5

Adaptability and Flexibility

Hello again, my dear apprentices! I see that you are eager to learn, and that brings me great joy. It is a delight for any gardener to watch the flowers he has watered grow and bloom. It's the same with teachers and their students. Speaking of flowers, you must have noticed how much the valley has blossomed after yesterday's rain. Such is the power of water. It can bring life, and it can also take it away. It is a tremendous force to be reckoned with.

On your way home after school, stop at the red bridge and contemplate the river for a while. It flows so calmly, yet it digs valleys and canyons at the same time. It smooths the rough stones and always reaches its goal. It can carve or even move the rocks, but it can also go around them. You can't stop it or close it off. If you block it, it will find another way. It will go around your obstacle, overflow if it has to, but still get where it's going. Its power lies in its flexibility and adaptability. We can use these qualities in our battles as well.

"Water shapes its course according to the nature of the ground over which it flows. The soldier works out his victory in relation to the foe whom he is facing."

Think about it! If you were building a house, would you use only a hammer? Or you would use a different tool for each task. You would need to use a hammer for the nails. But also a chisel for the stones, a trowel for the cement, a shovel for the sand, a leveler for the bricks, and so on. The tools themselves don't do the job. You do. You achieve your goal using different tools, materials, and approach for each part of the process. You adapt by staying flexible.

Say you have different math and English teachers. Your math teacher might be strict about getting homework done on time. Your English teacher, on the other hand, focuses more on creativity and less on deadlines. To succeed, you need to adapt. Always turn in your math homework on time. But be more creative and maybe a little less strict with deadlines in English.

If you play sports, consider changing your approach based on your opponent. Let's say a basketball team plays aggressive defense. In this case, you should practice shooting from a distance to counter it.

When it comes to friends, they may need different kinds of support. One may appreciate direct advice when facing a problem, while another may prefer to just have someone who listens. Consider what each friend needs, and you'll have stronger friendships.

Being adaptable and flexible also means being prepared to change your plans when the unexpected happens. Like water, you can find new paths around the rocks in your journey.

You know that I like to spice up my lectures with war stories from times long gone. So here's another one. Many centuries ago, there lived a brave Thracian[1] soldier named Spartacus. He had the ill fate of being enslaved by the Romans and sent to a gladiator

---

[1] **The Thracians** were a group of ancient people. They lived in a region called Thrace, which is now part of modern-day Bulgaria, Greece, and Turkey. They were known for their fierce warriors, and many Thracians, like Spartacus, were captured and forced to fight as gladiators in the Roman Empire. Despite being overshadowed by larger civilizations like the Romans and Greeks, the Thracians had a rich culture with their own language, art, and customs.

school [2]. You wouldn't be wrong if you guessed that his life was miserable. Every day, he had to endure relentless, back-breaking training, only to be thrown into deadly battles in the arena. As if that wasn't enough, the owner of the school was a ruthless master who treated his slaves abominably.

But despite the terrible circumstances, Spartacus did not despair. He decided to use what little he had to improve his lot. *"But General Sun, he had nothing,"* - you might say. *"Not even himself. He was the property of another."* Here, you would be wrong, my dear students. Spartacus may have been a slave, but he still had his sharp mind. His ability to adapt to difficult situations was his invisible weapon that no one could take away. Using it, he quickly ranked among the best gladiators and earned their respect.

Not long after, he and his comrades in arms decided to attempt an escape. However, to do that, they needed weaponry, which they didn't have. Spartacus and the other gladiators found a way around this by seizing whatever they could find in the kitchen. Choppers, knives, and spits became their armament. With these, they fought their way out of the gladiator school. Their former master quickly gathered a small force to recapture them, but Spartacus outwitted and crushed it, taking the soldiers' weapons and armor. Now that Spartacus' band was well equipped with their enemy's battle gear, they resembled a small army.

---

[2] *Gladiator school*: In ancient Rome, a gladiator school (called a ludus) was a place where enslaved people, prisoners of war, or volunteers trained to become gladiators. Gladiators were fighters who entertained crowds by battling in arenas like the famous Colosseum. At the school, they trained in different fighting styles and with various weapons under the supervision of a lanista, the manager, or owner of the school. Life at the gladiator school was harsh, with brutal training and strict discipline. But some gladiators became famous and earned the admiration of the public.

Soon, other slaves in the area heard about Spartacus' resourcefulness and joined him. That's how his rebellion against the mighty Roman Empire began. The Roman Senate[3] acted swiftly. They sent a well-armed force to put down the uprising. Spartacus realized the likelihood of losing the battle was high, so he withdrew his men to the nearby Mount Vesuvius[4]. His quick wit saved him and his men once more.

[3] **The Roman Senate** was a council of powerful government officials who made important decisions about the state. It consisted of wealthy and influential men, usually from noble families, who served for life. The Senate advised Roman leaders, passed laws, and controlled finances, foreign policy, and the military. While the Senate was very powerful during the Roman Republic, its influence declined when emperors took control during the Roman Empire. However, it remained an important symbol of Roman politics and tradition throughout Rome's history.

[4] **Mount Vesuvius** is a famous volcano in Italy. It is best known for its catastrophic eruption in 79 AD that buried the Roman cities of Pompeii and Herculaneum under ash and lava. Located near the modern city of Naples, Vesuvius is one of the most dangerous volcanoes in the world because it is still active, and millions of people live nearby. Despite its deadly history, it is also an important symbol in Roman history, and its fertile soil makes the surrounding land good for farming. Vesuvius has erupted many times since 79 AD, but that eruption remains one of the most well-known natural disasters in history.

However, the Romans did not give up the chase. They blocked the rebels' way of retreat, thinking they had them cornered. But again, they underestimated Spartacus' adaptability and resourcefulness. Rather than waiting to be starved out or fighting a hopeless battle, Spartacus used the land to his advantage. He ordered his men to make ropes and long ladders from the vines and trees growing on the mountain. Then, under the cover of night, the rebels used them to climb down the cliffs on the other side of Vesuvius. The Romans hadn't guarded this side because they believed it was impassable. Spartacus and his men safely reached the ground and launched a surprise attack on their enemy from behind. The Roman soldiers, confident they had everything under control, were caught completely off guard.

Once again, Spartacus' adaptability and flexibility allowed him to turn a dangerous situation into a victory. His willingness to change his strategy based on the circumstances helped him outsmart the Romans and continue his fight for freedom.

Learn from this story and take this to heart: Always be like water. Adapt your strategies to the challenges you face, whether in war, in the classroom, or with friends. Understand your environment. Know the strengths and weaknesses of those around you. Then, adjust your approach accordingly. Flexibility and adaptability are the keys to overcoming obstacles and achieving your goals.

Being flexible and adaptable also involves learning from your mistakes. Mistakes bring experience, and experience gives you the knowledge of what to do and what not to do in the future. Flexibility is about having the strength and wisdom to change your plan if needed. When you fail, instead of giving up, find a new way to accomplish your objective. Remember, young warriors: To be rigid is to be fragile, but to be flexible is to be unstoppable.

With that, we finish the lesson. In the late afternoon, as you pass by the river on your way home, recall what I taught you. Then ponder these questions: When was the last time you had to adapt to an unexpected situation? How can you use the principle of adaptability and flexibility to turn challenges into opportunities?

Now go, and I will meet you again in the next session.

Class dismissed.

Chapter 6

Using Deception Wisely

A h, my dear disciples! I am so glad to see you again, as I almost got late for our class today. If you are wondering why, I'll tell you, for it is a good story. It begins with our local Governor, Liang Junyu. He heard that I teach at this school, and he couldn't wait to see me. Many years ago, he was also a student of mine and a very bright one. Thanks to my teaching, he made a successful career in the army and later in government. Someone told him that his favorite teacher, General Sun Tzu, was here, and he rushed to meet me early in the morning.

The Governor came to my secluded rural home but missed me by 10 or 15 minutes, for I always leave a little early. He and his assistant went after me, but as they passed by the river, they were attacked by a brown bear. They ran, but Governor Liang stumbled and fell to the ground. His assistant got too scared and, in his panic, he didn't notice that his master was no longer running with him. The assistant was still shaking when he found me on my way here. He told me what had happened, and we rushed back to help the Governor.

When we saw him, he was still lying flat on the ground, his feet slightly spread and his hands covering his neck and head. He looked dead, but there was no blood or other signs of struggle. His assistant started to cry. Then suddenly, Governor Liang jumped up. He was excited and in perfect health. *"Thank you, General Sun Tzu!"* - he said. *"You just saved my life."*

"Saved your life?" - I replied. *"I just came here, my dear friend. I didn't even see the bear. She was gone before we arrived."*

"You saved me with your teachings, my dear General Sun." - said the Governor and continued: *"The moment that bear appeared before us, I realized we wouldn't stand a chance if we fought her. So, I started thinking of another way out. The first thing that came to my mind was your lesson on deception. It all happened in a matter of seconds. I remembered that brown bears don't eat dead animals, and I took action immediately. I pretended to stumble and die to buy some time for my assistant to escape. The bear rushed toward me, but when she saw my motionless body, she was surprised and started to sniff me. She tried to turn me over to check me, but I anticipated that and spread my legs a bit, so she couldn't. I also covered my head and neck with my hands, thinking these were my weak spots in the current situation. The bear continued*

to examine me for some time. When she was completely convinced that I was indeed dead, she left. I won this battle all thanks to your teachings on the strategic use of deception."

Remember this, my dear students:

"All warfare is based on deception."

But fear not, for this is not a lesson in dishonesty. It's a lesson on the strategic use of surprise, illusion, and the element of the unexpected in overcoming challenges.

In strategy, deception is about outsmarting your opponent. It is about making them think you will do one thing while you plan to do another. It is about hiding your strength, overexposing your weakness, biding your time, and concealing your true intentions. It is also about being several steps ahead, guiding your rival's expectations to your advantage.

However, it's crucial to understand the difference between strategic deception and dishonesty. The former is a tool in games, competitions, and warfare. The latter has no place in the life of an honorable warrior. The line between the two may seem thin at first glance, but it isn't. Consider the chameleon, a master of natural deception. It changes its color not out of malice but to protect itself or to catch its prey. In some sports, athletes use feints or fake moves not to cheat but as a part of the game, adding depth and skill to the play.

Did you know that even in warfare, there are rules? They are known as "the laws of war" or "international humanitarian law" (IHL). Their primary purpose is to minimize the harm caused to civilians and to avoid unnecessary suffering and cruelty to soldiers. These rules are outlined in various international treaties and agreements, most notably the Geneva Conventions. Simply put, in war, you can use deception, but you are not allowed to use dishonesty or cruelty.

Speaking of deception, let me share a tale from the Three Kingdoms era[1]: A story of cunning and intellect that transcends the mere clashing of swords. It is the legend of Zhuge Liang and the Empty Fort Strategy, where deception turned the tide against overwhelming odds. In the midst of a turbulent campaign, Zhuge Liang, the famed strategist of the Shu Han Kingdom, found himself in a precarious situation. The city of Xicheng lay exposed, defended by only a handful of loyal soldiers.

Meanwhile, the formidable enemy general, Sima Yi, marched towards it. He led an army so vast it seemed to stretch to the horizon. Zhuge Liang knew his small force couldn't withstand a direct attack, so he devised a bold and audacious plan. As the enemy drew nearer, he ordered the city gates to be opened. He dressed his men as civilians and commanded them to sweep the streets. Zhuge Liang, also attired in civilian clothes, climbed up to the top of the city wall. There, in full view of the approaching enemy, he sat, calmly playing his guqin[2]. His fingers moved gracefully over the strings. Serene and melodic notes floated through the air.

---

[1] *The Three Kingdoms era* (220–280 AD) was a period in Chinese history. It was marked by the fragmentation of the Han dynasty into three rival states: Wei, Shu Han, and Wu. This period is famous for its intense wars and complex politics. It is also known for the strategic brilliance of key historical figures, such as Cao Cao, Liu Bei, Sun Quan, and Zhuge Liang. The events of this period were later romanticized in the classical Chinese novel - Romance of the Three Kingdoms. It blends historical facts with legend and folklore. To this day, it is one of the most beloved literary works in Chinese culture.

[2] *Guqin* is a traditional Chinese stringed instrument.

When Sima Yi's troops arrived, they encountered an unexpected sight. Confused, they stopped in their tracks. The wide open gates, the carefree civilians, and Zhuge Liang's calm demeanor struck a chord of deep unease. Sima Yi, a seasoned and cautious general, sensed a trap. Why else would Zhuge Liang, a master tactician, expose himself so vulnerable? It must be because he had a hidden army ready to pounce.

Suspicion gnawed at Sima Yi. He ordered his men to stand vigilant and observe. The guqin's haunting melody filled the silence. Each note was a challenge, each chord a declaration of confidence. The open gates seemed to mock the invaders, daring them to enter. *"Surely, this must be a trick,"* Sima Yi thought. *"A trap set by Zhuge Liang to lure us into an ambush."* Fearing an unseen danger, Sima Yi hesitated. The more he watched Zhuge Liang's calm performance, the more convinced he became that an attack would lead to disaster. Reluctantly, he ordered a retreat, unwilling to risk his men in what he believed was an ambush.

As the enemy withdrew, Zhuge Liang kept playing. His serene expression never faltered. His ruse had worked perfectly. He turned the very idea of fear against his foes. He outwitted a vastly superior force without spilling a single drop of blood. This tale, my dear students, illustrates the power of deception. Zhuge Liang understood that in war, as in all challenges, the direct approach sometimes yields to the cunning of the indirect. By deceiving his enemy, he eliminated their numerical superiority and their confidence. His own small numbers turned into a source of confusion.

Now, my dear warriors, it's time to contemplate our lesson. Can you think of a situation where it might be a good idea to appear weak when you're strong or strong when you're weak? What are some other ways in which you can confuse your opponents without lying or breaking the rules? Ponder on these questions, and let's take a break until the next lesson.

Class dismissed.

Chapter 7

The Importance of Preparation

Good day, my dear students! I'm glad to see you again after the short holiday. I hope you've spent some quality time with your families during the Qingming Festival[1]. Before we continue with another lesson on the art of war, let me ask you a simple question: Do you feel safe here? Yes? Why? Mhmm... I

---

[1] **Qingming Festival**, also called Tomb Sweeping Day, is when Chinese people honor their ancestors. They visit their graves, clean the sites, and make ritual offerings. It is not only a time of remembrance but also a celebration of the coming of spring. Many people honor the holiday by doing outdoor activities such as kite flying. It takes place on April 4th or 5th, depending on the solar calendar.

see... OK! Good answers! Indeed, you feel safe because our town is well fortified and guarded by soldiers. Not only that, but the Great Wall is nearby. It protects the entire valley from the raids of invaders. Even our school is surrounded by walls, and we are ready to defend it at any moment.

My dear apprentices, you feel safe because we are prepared. Long before any enemy threat, our beloved Governor readied the town for such. Our wise Emperor did the same by erecting the Great Wall. Our granaries are full. Our citizens are well-trained. They know what to do in case of foreign aggression. That's what gives us confidence that we can survive and thrive. It is also what deters our adversaries from even attempting to invade. Preparation, my young warriors, is the cornerstone of victory. Winners are always those who are better prepared. Remember this:

"The general who wins the battle makes many calculations in his temple before the battle is fought. The general who loses makes but few calculations beforehand."

Preparation is about laying the groundwork for success. You do this long before the challenge arrives. It's about foresight. About anticipating what's to come and readying yourself for it. A well-prepared individual is like a fortress —solid and unshakable. Not because he cannot be challenged but because he is ready for any challenge.

Did you know, my fellow scholars, that one of the strongest creatures on the planet is the ant? They may be tiny, but they are so mighty that they can lift objects up to a hundred times their body weight. It's like you being able to lift a car with your bare hands. Ants are strong, hardworking, and great at collaborating. That's why they are one of the most thriving groups of animals in the world. But do you know what's even more impressive about ants than their strength? They are exceptional at preparation. For example, ants are great at storing food. Some species, like the leafcutter ant, cut off pieces of leaves to bring back to their colonies. They don't eat these leaves. Instead, they use them to cultivate fungus gardens—their primary food source. That is how they ensure a continuous food supply. It's a complex form of agriculture that shows a high level of preparation and social organization.

Spiders are also great at preparation. They catch their victims not by chasing them but by crafting intricate webs. The design and location of these webs are critical. Spiders choose sites where insects are likely to travel. This preparation lets them capture prey efficiently. It ensures a steady food supply without spending energy on active hunting.

Preparation is as relevant for us humans as it is for animals. Let me tell you a story about two explorers who set out to reach the South Pole in 1911. Their names were Roald Amundsen and Robert Falcon Scott. Both men were determined, but their fates were very different due to their level of preparation.

Amundsen, a Norwegian explorer, planned his expedition meticulously. He went to live with the Inuit[2] people to learn from them how to survive in extreme cold. There, Amundsen acquired invaluable knowledge. He learned about the importance of fur clothing for warmth, techniques for building effective shelters, the benefits of a high-fat diet for energy in freezing temperatures, strategies for mental resilience, and practices for navigation in challenging environments. He also observed and adopted the Inuit's methods of using sled dogs, which were very well suited for the harsh conditions of the South Pole. Besides acquiring knowledge, Amundsen carefully calculated the food, clothing, and shelter his team would need. Thanks to his thorough

---

[2] **The Inuit** are Indigenous people who primarily live in the Arctic regions of Canada, Greenland, and Alaska. Traditionally, they were hunters, relying on animals like seals, whales, and caribou for food, clothing, and materials to build tools. The Inuit are known for their deep connection to the land and sea, and for living in one of the harshest environments on Earth. They built igloos (snow houses) in the winter and traveled using dog sleds. Today, many Inuit continue to maintain their cultural traditions while living in modern communities.

preparation, he and his team reached the South Pole first and returned safely.

In contrast, Robert Falcon Scott, a British Royal Navy officer, was less prepared. His team used ponies and motor sledges, which proved unreliable in the harsh Antarctic conditions. Additionally, they were less equipped to handle the extreme cold, and their food supplies were not well-planned.

Amundsen's team reached the South Pole on December 14, 1911, and returned safely. Scott's team arrived at the Pole on January 17, 1912, only to discover that Amundsen had beaten them. Tragically, Scott and his four companions perished on the return journey due to the harsh conditions and insufficient preparation.

The takeaway from this story is that success comes down to who is better prepared.

One very useful aspect of preparation is practicing. A great warrior once said:

"I fear not the man who has practiced 10,000 kicks once, but I fear the one who has practiced one kick 10,000 times."[3]

What he meant was that practice is a big part of preparation. The more you practice, the better your skills and your chances for a swift victory.

---

[3] **This quote** is from Bruce Lee, a renowned martial artist, actor, and philosopher. He is famous for his deep impact on martial arts. The quote shows that mastery of one skill is better than a shallow knowledge of many. It highlights Bruce Lee's belief in the power of refined techniques.

In your life, preparation takes many forms. It can be studying for your exams weeks in advance, not the night before. Or practicing your free throws repeatedly so that when the game is on the line, you're ready. Or rehearsing your lines for the school play until they become part of you.

Preparation is not just about the big moments. It's in the small, daily routines, in the habits you form, and in the discipline you build. It's about being prepared not only for the battles you expect but also for the unforeseen ones. Remember, young warriors: The battle is won long before it is fought. It's won in the quiet hours of preparation and in the commitment to readiness.

As we conclude this lesson, consider this: What are you preparing for right now? How can you improve your preparation? What habits can you develop today that will prepare you for the challenges ahead? Contemplate these questions, and I'll meet you again in the next lesson.

Class dismissed.

Chapter 8

The Art of Leadership

Greetings, my dear pupils! I have a quick question: Which of you has seen a dragon? What? No one? That's strange. Do you want to see one right now? OK, please follow me to the courtyard, where that small, square-shaped pond is. You know…

the one with the colorful koi fish... and that large statue of an imperial dragon in the middle.

I thought you hung around it every day during the breaks. How come you didn't see it? Oh, you thought I was talking about a real dragon... Well, we Chinese believe that dragons are shapeshifters, so it might be a little hard to spot a real one. They are too good at keeping a low profile and rarely reveal themselves. So for now, let's look at this one, made of bronze. He looks like he emerged from the pond to watch over our school. What a magnificent beast!

Dragons are perceived in various ways across different cultures. In many countries, they are considered evil monsters. It's the opposite in China. Here, dragons are a powerful symbol of leadership, authority, and strength. Who can tell me what leadership is? Yes, young lady? That's right! Leadership is the ability to guide and inspire a group of people to achieve a common goal.

At the top of every organization, there is a leader. The better the leader, the more successful the organization. What is an organization, you ask? It is a group of people who work toward a shared objective. The army is an organization. So are the state, the school, a sports team, an orchestra, a business, a corporation, and so on.

Most of the time, leaders are appointed. We call those "formal leaders." But some leaders emerge naturally, based on their qualities, skills, and charisma. These are known as "informal leaders." People just trust and follow them because of who they are. Informal leaders often get noticed and then promoted to formal positions. For example, you may be a leader in your soccer team without anyone appointing you (informal leader). Then, the coach may notice your leadership skills and make you the team captain (formal leader).

So, what qualities should a good leader possess? Who can tell me? Yes, young warrior? Strength and bravery? These are good traits, no doubt. They are essential for a hero. But not every hero can become a leader. Heroes often achieve feats alone, but leaders must be team players. They need to think not just for themselves but for their entire team. For that, they need a different, or better yet, an extended set of qualities. The dragon, especially the imperial dragon, represents those qualities, for he is the ultimate symbol of a wise and benevolent leader. Let's talk about them.

Look at the statue again. Do you see the giant pearl that the dragon holds? It symbolizes **WISDOM**. Wisdom is the ability to think deeply, to understand people and situations, and to make the right decisions at the right time. Just like the dragon, a wise leader holds the power of knowledge, always seeking to learn and grow. Wisdom allows leaders to grasp the complexities of situations and to strategize effectively.

Now, observe the dragon's eyes—sharp and focused, gazing into the distance. This represents **VISION**. A great leader has a clear idea of the future and guides their people toward it. Vision allows a leader to plan ahead and inspire others to follow their path.

INSPIRATION is another essential quality of true leaders. They inspire their team with their vision, the strength of their character, and most importantly, with their deeds.

"A leader leads by example, not by force."

True leaders live the values they preach, earning respect through their actions. They stand with their troops, not behind them, sharing both hardships and triumphs. Leaders inspire excitement about taking on challenges together. They make each person feel like they're part of something big and significant.

Come closer to the statue, please. Observe the dragon's open mouth, as if he's about to speak. What do you think he would say if he could? We speak what we think, right? So how do great leaders think? Hm? They think and act with **SINCERITY**. A leader must be honest and genuine in their words and actions. Sincerity builds trust, and trust is the foundation of any strong relationship, whether it's within a team, a community, or a whole nation.

Now step back and take a look at the entire pond. The tiled edges hold the water, but they also represent the borders of the dragon's realm. These motley koi fish are his subjects. Notice how the dragon seems to protect the pond with its coiled body. This is a symbol of **BENEVOLENCE**. A great leader must care for their people, showing kindness and compassion. Just as the dragon guards the pond, a leader must protect and nurture their team, ensuring that everyone feels valued and supported. Benevolence is most effective when paired with sincerity.

What else? Earlier, someone mentioned bravery. Bravery is the ability to face danger or pain without fear. Brave people often act without considering the risks because they fear nothing. However, it is different with **COURAGE**. Courage is about making a deliberate choice to act, even when you are afraid. It doesn't imply the absence of fear but rather the strength to overcome it.

While bravery can be instinctive, courage requires thought and determination. A courageous leader faces challenges head-on, even when the path is uncertain or risky. They understand the dangers but choose to act for the greater good. Courage isn't just about bold actions. It's also about making tough decisions and standing firm in difficult situations. A leader with courage inspires others to do the same. They show that with determination, any challenge can be met.

Another very important quality of a great leader is **DISCIPLINE**. It is the foundation of a leader's character. Discipline ensures that a leader stays focused and committed, even when faced with challenges. A disciplined leader follows through on their plans, and sets a strong example for others to follow. Discipline also involves self-control, enabling a leader to remain calm and make rational decisions under pressure. Without discipline, even the best strategies can fail.

Notice the dragon's coiled body. It is firm yet flexible, ready to move in any direction. It glides seamlessly between water, earth, and sky, adapting to its surroundings. This represents **ADAPTABILITY AND FLEXIBILITY**. A leader must be able to adjust their plans as circumstances change, much like the dragon shifts his form to navigate through different environments. Flexibility allows a leader to find new solutions when faced with unexpected challenges.

By now, you must have noticed that all these qualities intertwine, complement each other, and work in sync. Each one is connected and depends on the rest. Beyond embodying them, a true leader must also know how to balance them. Only then can they inspire trust, loyalty, and respect, while effectively guiding their followers to achieve success.

While we are still admiring the dragon statue and contemplating leadership, let's explore some examples of great leaders from different walks of life. Here are some of my favorites:

Jesus Christ - Spiritual Leader

Jesus Christ is the central figure in Christianity. He is revered as one of the most influential spiritual leaders in history. His teachings were on love, compassion, and forgiveness. They shaped the morals and ethics of billions. Jesus led by example. He lived the principles he preached. He inspired his disciples to spread his teachings throughout the world. His parables and life lessons were on humility and service. They continue to inspire acts of charity and peace for millennia after his time.

Queen Elizabeth I - The Unifier of a Nation

Queen Elizabeth I of England was famous for her strong and effective rule. She led during a time of religious conflict and political instability. Her leadership ushered in the Elizabethan era. It was marked by the defeat of the Spanish Armada[1]. It was also marked by the flourishing of English culture and the rise of England as a great European power. Her Majesty possessed exceptional political skills. She inspired loyalty and had a vision of a united England. Thanks to these qualities, Queen Elizabeth I is remembered as one of the greatest leaders in history.

Sheikh Zayed bin Sultan Al Nahyan - Visionary Builder

Sheikh Zayed bin Sultan Al Nahyan was the founder of the United Arab Emirates. He turned a group of desert villages into a modern, prosperous country. His vision extended beyond the vast oil riches. His Highness invested in infrastructure, education, and healthcare. He laid the foundations for the diverse and stable

---

[1] *The Spanish Armada* was a large fleet of ships sent by Spain to invade England in 1588. The English Navy, led by Queen Elizabeth I, defeated the Armada despite being outnumbered. This victory was vital for England. It saved it from being invaded and helped establish it as a powerful nation.

country that we see today. Sheikh Zayed was renowned for his wisdom and foresight. He cared about the environment and sustainable development[2] long before they became global priorities. His diplomatic skills unified the Emirates and made them a significant player in world affairs. Sheikh Zayed led with pragmatism, generosity, and a deep commitment to his people's welfare.

Mahatma Gandhi - Revolutionary Leader

Mahatma Gandhi is often called the Father of the Indian Nation. He demonstrated that leaders can be peaceful and still make a significant change. His strategy of nonviolent resistance led India to freedom from British rule. Gandhi was committed to peace, truth, and justice. His dedication inspired movements for civil rights and freedom across the world. Gandhi led a peaceful revolution. He showed outstanding leadership and strategy. Mahatma Gandhi used moral force to overcome colonial power.

---

[2] **Sustainable development** means using what we need now without hurting the ability of future generations to get what they need. It involves using resources wisely and protecting the environment. This way, we can have a healthy planet and enough resources for everyone, now and in the future.

Steve Jobs - Business Innovator

Steve Jobs co-founded Apple Inc. and revolutionized several industries, including computers, smartphones, animated movies, music, and digital publishing. He combined visionary thinking with exceptional resourcefulness. He foresaw the impact of design on technology. Mr. Jobs led by

example, always pushing for product excellence. His leadership transformed Apple into one of the world's most valuable companies. Steve Jobs demonstrated that a clear vision and creative thinking can lead to remarkable success.

Many more great leaders deserve to be studied and emulated. Indeed, this subject could fill an entire book. Notice how each leader honed and utilized a distinct quality from the list we discussed. Some excelled in adaptability, others in compassion. Some were outstanding in strategic thinking, while others were exceptional at maintaining calm. However, each also possessed the other key qualities to some degree.

Even in the animal kingdom, there are leaders and followers.

Take lions, for example. Their prides are led by a dominant male, often called the alpha male. He uses his strength, experience, and strategic thinking to protect and guide the others. His leadership is not about bullying or being bossy. It's about ensuring the safety and well-being of all the group's members. The alpha male leads by example, showing bravery in battles and making wise decisions about when and where to hunt. He earns the respect and trust of the pride not through force alone, but by being a dependable leader who looks after his family.

Elephant herds, unlike lion prides, are matriarchal. They are led by the eldest female, the matriarch[3]. She uses her knowledge of migration routes, waterholes, and food sources to guide her herd

---

[3] **Matriarchy** is a family or group in which the mothers, grandmothers, or other adult women are in charge. They make the big decisions and lead the group. It is the opposite of a patriarchy, where the fathers or other adult males are in charge. In some animal groups and human cultures, the oldest females lead, and everyone follows their rules.

safely across vast areas. Her memory and experience are vital during the dry season when resources are scarce. She leads with wisdom and foresight.

Even underwater, many animals rely on their leaders for guidance. Dolphin pods, for instance, are led by strong individuals. These alpha leaders guide the group through treacherous waters and coordinate hunting efforts. They also protect the pod from threats such as predators. Dolphin leaders exhibit great communication skills and strong social bonds. They always put the pod's welfare first.

We talked about great leaders and the qualities that made them such. We also discussed leadership in the animal kingdom. Now, let's see how all this can apply to you. In your life, you can show leadership in many ways. It could be by leading your sports team. Or you can take responsibility for a group project. You can organize a holiday celebration or family activity. Or you can take up a charitable initiative. You can also steer your friends and siblings away from a bad path by being a good example. Leadership can be found in small acts of kindness as well. It is in the courage to do what is right and in the discipline that allows you to pursue your goals, no matter what.

Now, I'd love to hear what's on your mind. In what ways do you think you can be a leader in your own life? How can you inspire, support, and guide others? And what leadership qualities do you need to develop?

While you ponder these questions, consider this: Leadership is not about giving orders. It's about caring for those under your command. You inspire them by personal example to give their best in achieving your common goal.

With this dragon pearl of wisdom, I leave you until our next lesson.

Class dismissed.

Chapter 9

Patience and Timing

Welcome, my dear scholars! Are you ready to learn? Good, good... I'm glad to see that you are so eager to study. Let's quench this noble thirst for knowledge.

Let me ask you this: Today, when you passed the red bridge on your way to school, you probably noticed those people standing there, catching fish with their rods. How are they doing it? And what are the most essential skills a fisherman must have? I would say patience and timing. Yes, you have to know the fish and your own skills. Yes, you have to be well-prepared and strategically positioned. And yes, you must know how to lure the fish. But all of this will be for nothing if you are not patient. You must sit still and wait as long as it takes for the fish to bite the hook. Then, you must be ready to act swiftly at the exact moment. All the waiting will be in vain if your timing is poor. Patience and timing are of vital importance. They matter not only for successful fishing but also for success in war and life in general.

Write this down:

"He who knows when he can fight and when he cannot will be victorious."

You see, my young scholars, patience is not merely waiting. It is about waiting with purpose and awareness. It's the quiet strength that allows you to observe and plan. Then comes timing. Timing means recognizing the right moment to act. It's that perfect moment when your actions will matter most.

Consider the lion, the king of the savanna. When hunting, he doesn't charge directly at the herd. Instead, he waits. Hidden in the bushes, the lion watches silently. He is choosing the right target and the right moment. His patience is strong, and his selection of when to strike is timed perfectly.

Even plants use patience and timing. Take the bamboo, for instance. In the Far East, we admire it for its strength and resilience. But do you know how bamboo grows? For the first few years, all you see is a tiny shoot. All of its growth happens underground. There, a complex root system spreads deep and wide. When it's ready, it shoots skyward with amazing speed. This is patience paired with timing. The bamboo waits until it is fully prepared to grow rapidly and securely. A wise leader knows that some efforts take time to mature. Like the bamboo, success comes all at once only after much groundwork.

But enough examples from flora[1] and fauna[2]. Let me share a true war story with you, for you know that, as a military general, I love to study warfare. It's about the siege of Tyre, and it goes like this: Once, there was a great king. His name was Alexander of Macedon, but he was known as Alexander the Great. In his quest to create an empire that spanned three continents, he came upon the city of Tyre. It was a strong island fortress in the Mediterranean Sea. Its walls were tall, and its soldiers brave. Tyre was considered impregnable with its well-planned naval defenses.

Alexander was aware of Tyre's strategic advantages. He knew a direct assault would be costly, so he devised an audacious plan. He decided to turn the island into a peninsula. To achieve this,

---

[1] *Flora* refers to all plant life in a specific area or time. It includes everything from tiny grasses to giant trees. Scientists study flora to understand the types of plants in different places and how they interact with their surroundings. For example, the flora of a rainforest includes many trees, ferns, and vines, forming a unique ecosystem.

[2] *Fauna* refers to all the animals found in a specific area or period. It includes everything from tiny insects to large mammals like elephants or whales. By studying fauna, scientists learn about the different kinds of animals in an ecosystem. They also discover how they interact with each other and their environment. For example, the fauna of the African savanna includes lions, elephants, zebras, and many types of birds and bugs. They all share the same habitat.

he ordered the building of a causeway[3] stretching from the mainland to the very foot of Tyre's fortress walls. After meticulous preparations, Alexander besieged the city and began construction. It was an engineering feat of enormous difficulty due to the depth of the sea and the attacks of Tyrian ships. The weeks turned into months. The Tyrians grew confident, believing that their city was unassailable. They launched sorties[4], setting fire to Alexander's siege engines. They thought they could outlast his patience, but Alexander was resolute. His response was to bring in more ships and turn the siege into a blockade. He sent in additional soldiers and engineers. He even commandeered the fleets of nearby cities he had subdued.

Alexander's patience was tested again and again. Countless setbacks came his way. But after each one, he adjusted his tactics accordingly and continued his relentless pursuit. After seven grueling months, the causeway was completed. Alexander's catapults were now within range. When his troops could finally breach the walls at close range, he ordered the assault.

The fall of Tyre was a testament to Alexander's understanding of patience and timing. He waited until his preparations were in place and the morale within Tyre had been eroded. Then, he took the city with decisive and swift action. This reduced losses to his forces and despaired his opponents.

---

[3] *A causeway* is an elevated road or path that crosses wet ground or water. It is usually made of compacted earth, stone, or sometimes even wood. Some areas are hard to travel through due to water or marsh. Causeways are built to make crossing over such areas easier for people and vehicles. For example, a causeway may connect an island to the mainland or cross a flooded area.

[4] *Sortie* is an attack by troops coming out from a defensive position.

Remember, young warriors: Patience is not inaction. It is calculated action. It's about knowing that sometimes, the most powerful thing you can do is wait and watch. And when the moment is right, act with precision and purpose.

In your world, this principle applies in many ways.

Say you are making a cake. You have to mix the ingredients well and bake it for the right amount of time. If you are patient and follow the recipe, the cake will come out delicious. But if you hurry and take it out too early, it might be undercooked and not tasty at all. So, patience and timing are key to cooking.

Or think about saving up for something you really want, like a new bike or a video game. It takes time to salt away enough money, and you must be patient. You might have to save your allowance for many months. During this time, you learn the importance of patience and develop the discipline of resisting unnecessary purchases. When you finally save enough and buy what you want, it feels much more rewarding. It is because you were patient and waited for the right moment to spend your money.

Mastering patience and timing can pave your way to success, no matter what battlefield you choose to conquer.

A great philosopher once posed this question:

"Do you have the patience to wait till your mud settles and the water is clear? Can you remain unmoving till the right action arises by itself?"[5]

In essence, he was asking whether you can be patient enough to let things calm down. Can you wait until the situation becomes clear, and act only when the time is right? The quote is about trusting that sometimes the best action is no action. Instead, you should wait for the right moment when your path forward will reveal itself naturally.

Reflect on this as you walk back across the red bridge today. Then, think if there are areas in your life, where you need to be more patient and wait for the right moment.

Class dismissed.

---

[5] This quote is credited to Lao Tzu, an ancient Chinese philosopher who lived more than 2,500 years ago. He wrote Tao Te Ching, a famous text that introduced the ideas of Taoism. Taoism is a philosophy that promotes living in harmony with nature and the "Tao" or "The Way." Lao Tzu's teachings are on simplicity, patience, and compassion. His ideas have influenced the thinking of many people around the world about life and nature.

Chapter 10

Applying the Art of War

知識就是力量

W ell met, my dear disciples! I am glad to see you again in this beautiful place of learning that is our school's courtyard. Isn't it interesting how time flies when you're having fun? It seems like only yesterday when we had our first lesson under the shade of that big ginkgo tree. Since then, I've taught you all of the important lessons from *the Art of War*. I hope to have kindled the fire that burns in the heart of every winner. Armed with this knowledge, now you graduate. There will be no final exam today, but life will test you often throughout your journey.

Wisdom doesn't come from the mere acquisition of information. You have the knowledge, and now you need experience, which is equally important.

"But, General Sun Tzu, how does one gain experience?" - you probably wonder. Experience comes not only from dealing with real-life situations but also from preparation. Consider how kittens practice catching mice. They start by playing with balls of yarn. They also play with their parents' tails, with their siblings, and with anything else they can find. Long before they see a real mouse, they have practiced hunting through play. All baby animals learn this way: Not by making mistakes, which are often fatal in the wild, but by playing. Games are not to be underestimated. Even in warfare, there are military exercises, which are essentially games for soldiers. It's the same in almost all walks of life. Before adults get their driver's license, they learn how to drive in a safe environment. Pilots hone their skills not on real airplanes but on flight simulators. These are nothing but realistic video games. Dentists rehearse on dummies with fake teeth. Firefighters drill in specialized training facilities known as fire training centers. To be able to compete, athletes train in sports complexes for months and even years.

The more you practice, the better you become and the more experience you gain. Luckily, you are still young and have plenty of time ahead. It's up to you to take advantage of it and not waste it. You are like the little kittens now. You practice in the fairly safe environment that is your childhood. In this way, you prepare for the real-life situations you will face in the future.

What to practice, you ask? Practice using the principles that I have taught you. Contemplate them, and think about how you can apply them in your daily life. Then, do it.

Don't be afraid of failure. Failing is part of practice and a very important one. You will fail many times during your life's journey, and that's OK. You'll probably learn even more from your failures than from your successes. Remember, young warriors—NEVER allow your failures to make you give up and despair. When you fail, accept it as just a temporary defeat. Then, get back up and continue the fight.

The wise Confucius[1] once said:

"A man is great not because he hasn't failed; a man is great because failure hasn't stopped him."

Be great, my friends!

Now, let's revisit the principles of winning one last time. Here are the most essential among them. You should develop these by putting them into practice.

- **Practice strategic planning.** Plan your days, plan your weeks, plan your months, plan your years, plan your life. Being well-organized is a distinguishing trait of every winner. Write down your plans and make it a habit to read them often. Make a plan for tomorrow before you go to bed. Then, read your plan when you wake up. Make plans for specific projects, for your relationships, for your workouts, and so on. Set goals in your plans. Add deadlines to your goals. Last but not least, try to imagine that you have already achieved your goal and embrace the

---

[1] **Confucius** was a famous teacher, philosopher, and thinker in ancient China, born around 551 B.C. He is best known for his wise sayings and ideas about how people should live and treat each other. Confucius believed that respect for others (especially elders), honesty, and education were very important. His teachings have influenced Chinese culture for thousands of years and are still respected today.

satisfaction this brings. This powerful practice alone will draw you closer to success.

- **Practice self-reflection.** Analyze your behavior in different situations. Think about why you acted this way. Could you do it differently to achieve a better outcome? Find your weaknesses and get rid of them or reduce their impact. Find your strengths, develop them, and rely on them.

- **Learn to meditate and make it a habit.** Meditation clears your mind. It helps you see things distinctly and analyze them without bias. Feelings often get involved in real-life situations. Like when you argue with a friend, for example. They lead to bad decisions frequently. You don't see the real picture when you are under the influence of emotions because they cloud your judgment. After meditation, your mind is calm, and you see the situation without attachment. This leads to a better understanding of yourself and your rival, better decisions, and victory in the end.

- **Practice studying and analyzing your enemy.** By "enemy," I mean any challenge in life, whether it's an event, a process, or a person. An enemy can be math, which defeated you in your last exam. Study it well by reading the textbook. Then, practice what you learned by solving math problems. And in the next exam, crush it. If your foe is a person, try to understand their view. Put yourself in their shoes and see the situation through their eyes. When you truly understand your enemy, one of two things will happen. Either you will defeat them, or you will find a solution to their problem, and they will no longer be your enemy.

- **Practice winning without a fight.** Remember this:

"Victorious warriors win first and then go to war, while defeated warriors go to war first and then seek to win."

Think about how you can make your opponent give up before the fight. And why not even turn them into an ally? The best victories are the ones where everyone wins. Wouldn't it be great if that happened more often? Develop your skills to negotiate and forge alliances. These days, you may call these alliances friendships or partnerships. If you want something from your parents, negotiate with them. Offer something in return. For example, something you can do for them. Team up with your siblings and have them help you negotiate with your mom and dad. Maybe jointly you can make an offer that your parents can't refuse. That way, you'll win without a fight.

- **Practice being flexible and adaptable.** If things don't go as planned, switch to plan B. If that doesn't work either, try plan C. If there is an obstacle in your way, think of ways to get around it. Be like water and find the path of least resistance. If you plan to visit your grandparents, but the airport is closed due to bad weather, go by car. If that does not work, take the train. Or the bus. Or go by boat. There is usually more than one way to reach your goal in life. Being flexible and adaptable is the skill to find and use those ways.

- **Develop your leadership skills.** Some people are natural-born leaders, while others must learn how to become one. Talk to people, make friends, and care for them. Unite them around a common goal and guide them toward it. Lead by example. If you want your team to win the championship, practice more than anyone else, including your teammates. It will inspire them, and they will look up to you. Then, devise a winning strategy for each game or help your coach apply his. If there is a school project, read more on the subject than anyone else. Talk to your teacher and your parents about it. Share the insights you've gained with the rest of your team. Then, suggest a plan and coordinate everyone's tasks. At home, become a role model for your brothers and sisters. Show them that you care about them, and they will gladly follow your lead.

- **Practice your discipline.** Don't let distractions take you off the path to success. Today, many temptations offer instant joy. Know that, in most cases, such temptations are bad for you. They usually end up costing you dearly later. Stay away from drugs, cigarettes, alcohol, and other addictive substances. Avoid eating junk food and limit screen time for TV, video games, tablets, and computers. Don't let short-term pleasures lead you to long-term pain. True happiness comes from achieving your goals. But mostly, it comes from becoming the person who can achieve them. The effort you put into pursuing your ambitions makes you a better person. This transformation feels far more rewarding than any short-term pleasure. Suppose you want to win a big national karate championship. You train every day for a long, long time. You turn yourself into a skilled martial artist. This gives you confidence, the respect of others, an athletic body, and many more amazing benefits. Yes, it will be fantastic to win that championship. But even if you don't - you still win. Your transformation into a great person is the ultimate prize. But to achieve it, you need discipline.

- **Another good habit you can develop is to study remarkable people.** This will benefit you greatly. Read their biographies. Watch movies about them. Try to study how they think, talk, and act. Then, reflect on what you learned and practice emulating them.

Speaking of biographies of remarkable achievers, let me share another story with you. Mine... You may already know something about me since you trusted me to be your teacher. But you can't know as much as I do, so listen, and you may learn something new. Maybe my life, work, and achievements will inspire you to walk confidently on your path to success.

I was born in the state of Qi during a time of chaos known in China as the Spring and Autumn period. My grandfather was a general who had fought in many wars. My father was a high-ranking official. My birth name was Sun Wu. Later in life, because of my achievements, people called me Sun Tzu, which means "Master Sun."

I inherited my interest in warfare from my father and grandfather, but the situation in our country also influenced me. At that time, it was in shambles. Four major clans[2] fought over land, taxes, people, and wealth. My family was caught in the crossfire, and we were at risk of becoming collateral damage[3]. Because of this, when I was in my twenties, we moved south to the safer state of Wu.

When we got there, I didn't rush to find a job. Instead, I chose to live in seclusion in the mountains outside the capital. There, I

---

[2] **Clan** is a close-knit group of people. They are part of an extended family and trace their ancestry to a common ancestor. Clans were very important in past societies, especially in Scotland and Ireland. Members of a clan shared the same last name. They lived in the same territory and were loyal to their clan's leader. They stood together and protected each other like one big family. Today, clans still exist in some places around the world.

[3] **Collateral Damage** means accidental harm or destruction. It happens in addition to the intended damage during a war or a fight. For example, when soldiers try to destroy an enemy hideout but accidentally damage nearby homes. The damage to those homes is collateral damage. It's an unfortunate result that leaders try to avoid or reduce as much as they can.

devoted myself to studying military strategies. I also observed the geopolitics[4] of the time. Over five years, I wrote a treatise[5] on warfare and the philosophy of winning. I titled it *The Art of War*.

[4] **Geopolitics studies** how geography, economics, and politics affect each other globally. It also examines how a country's land, resources, people, and politics affect its relations with other countries. Understanding geopolitics is important for world leaders. It's vital for their decisions about diplomacy, security, and international relations.
[5] **Treatise** is a very detailed guidebook on a specific topic written by an expert. For example, The Art of War by Sun Tzu is a treatise on military strategy. People use its lessons in many other fields, like sports and business.

During this time, I befriended a guy named Wu Zixu, who shared my interest in military tactics. Wu Zixu served under King Helü of Wu as an official in charge of the King's schedule. That's like a modern-day chief of staff. Later, thanks to my friend's recommendations, I presented *The Art of War* to the King. That's how I earned his admiration and an appointment as a general. Thanks to me, our small kingdom defeated our arch-enemy, the mighty state of Chu. We captured their capital and became a regional superpower.

I don't like to brag, but I am proud that in my 40 years as a military commander, I have never lost a single battle. I think that record speaks volumes about my martial skills. It also shows a deep understanding of people and conflict. I achieved this not by using brute force but by applying strategy and wisdom. I knew when to fight and when to avoid battle. And I always, always prepared meticulously.

I believe the supreme art of war is to subdue the enemy without fighting. This philosophy has endured for centuries. It has influenced thousands of people, many of whom are beyond the military. These include people from the world of business, sports, and personal development. Strategy is not limited to the battlefield. It is relevant to every challenge or goal you pursue. Life will test you in many ways. With a strategic approach, you can foresee likely problems, and you can prepare to overcome them before they arise."

Remember, young warriors: True wisdom is using knowledge with understanding. You've mastered how to be adaptable, prepared, and benevolent, and how to take calculated actions. These traits should guide you to victory in every endeavor. Don't just learn these teachings—put them into practice. Challenge yourself to think critically, act strategically, and lead with compassion.

The path you take is yours to choose. But keep in mind the guiding principles we have explored. They are your map and compass as you navigate the complex terrain of life. Go forth with courage and clarity, my friends. Make your journey one of impact, integrity, and, above all, wisdom.

Class is dismissed, but your learning has just begun. Embark on your journey with the art of strategy as your guide, and turn challenges into stepping stones on your path to success.

Farewell, young warriors, and may your paths always lead you to wisdom.

Outro

Hey Dear Reader,

Martin Malchev here—the author. The real one, not Sun Tzu...

Did you enjoy the book? If so, please consider writing a review so other readers can learn about it as well. And if you didn't like it - please slowly put the book down, and forget this ever happened. Just kidding! Bad reviews are welcome too. Kind of…

Also, I plan to turn this into a series, where many renowned historical figures share their wisdom with young readers like you. If you want to be notified when the second title is released, you can scan this QR code to subscribe to my email notifications.

Thanks for reading my book, and I hope to meet you again in the next one.

Best regards,

Martin Malchev